A ROOKIE READER

SOMETIMES THINGS CHANGE

By Patricia Eastman

Illustrations by Seymour Fleishman

Prepared under the direction of Robert Hillerich, Ph.D.

CHILDRENS PRESS ™

CHICAGO

Library of Congress Cataloging in Publication Data

Eastman, Patricia.
  Sometimes things change.

  (Rookie reader)
  Includes word list.
  Summary: Sometimes things change from what they were at first: a caterpillar becomes a butterfly, a trickle becomes a river, a word becomes a story, a stranger becomes a friend, and a baby becomes you.
  [1. Change — Fiction] I. Fleishman, Seymour, ill.
II. Title.   III. Series.
PZ7.E1315So   1983   [E]   83-10090
ISBN 0-516-02044-7

Sometimes things change.
Once upon a time
a butterfly...

3

was a caterpillar.

A frog...

was a tadpole.

A turtle...

7

was an egg.

Sometimes things change
from what they were at first.
Did you know that
once upon a time
a raisin…

9

was a grape?
It was.

A tree...

11

was a seed.

A flower...

13

was a bud.

You...

were a baby.

Sometimes things change
from what they were at first.
Did you know that
once upon a time
a river...

17

was a trickle?
It was.

A raindrop...

was an ocean.

A snowflake…

was a cloud.

Sometimes things change
from what they were at first.
Once upon a time
a song...

was a note.

A story...

25

was a word.

A picture...

was a line.

Sometimes things change
from what they were at first.
Did you know that
once upon a time
a friend...

29

was a stranger?
It's true.

WORD LIST

		story
a	grape	stranger
an	it	tadpole
at	it's	that
baby	know	they
bud	line	things
butterfly	note	time
caterpillar	ocean	tree
change	once	trickle
cloud	picture	true
did	raisin	turtle
egg	raindrop	upon
first	river	was
flower	seed	were
friend	snowflake	what
frog	sometimes	word
from	song	you

About the Author

Patricia Eastman was born in New York, but grew up in the northwest suburbs of Chicago. She started her writing in college, and her first published book, *Sometimes Things Change*, originated from a homework project. Pat's major was Early Childhood Education and she is currently working on establishing her own day-care center. Although she doesn't have any children of her own, she loves the preschoolers. Patricia's interests are music, eating, cooking, skiing, traveling, and drama.

About the Artist

Seymour Fleishman has illustrated more than fifty children's books, several of which he also wrote. He and his wife Esther live with their dog (whose breed is uncertain) in a big, old Victorian house in Chicago. They have two grown daughters. In his spare time, Mr. Fleishman enjoys gardening, doing carpentry work around the house, and camping.